New England

A
PHOTOGRAPHIC
PORTRAIT

J. DENNIS ROBINSON

First published in the United States
of America by:

Twin Lights Publishers, Inc.
10 Hale Street
Rockport, Massachusetts 01966
Telephone: (978) 546-7398
http://www.twinlightspub.com

ISBN 1-885435-39-8

10 9 8 7 6 5 4

Book design by
SYP Design & Production, Inc.
http://www.sypdesign.com

Printed in China

Other titles in the Photographic Portrait
series:

Cape Ann
Kittery to the Kennebunks
The Mystic Coast, Stonington to New London
The White Mountains
Boston's South Shore
Upper Cape Cod
The Rhode Island Coast
Greater Newburyport
Portsmouth and Coastal New Hampshire
Naples, Florida
Sarasota, Florida
The British Virgin Islands
Portland, Maine
Mid and Lower Cape Cod
The Berkshires
Boston
Camden, Maine
Sanibel and Captiva Islands
San Diego's North County Coast
Newport Beach, California
Phoenix and the Valley of the Sun
Wasatch Mountains, Utah
The Florida Keys
Miami and South Beach
Maryland's Eastern Shore
Asheville, North Carolina
Charleston, South Carolina
Savannah, Georgia
Southeastern Arizona
The United States Virgin Islands
Massachusetts

Contents

Connecticut 8

Rhode Island 28

Massachusetts 44

New Hampshire 68

Maine 92

Vermont 110

Introduction

In your first puzzle map of America, New England was likely a single piece—an indistinct lump of wood or cardboard that tucked neatly in the upper right corner of the nation. The six sliver-sized states were simply too small for your tiny hand to manage. But already images of New England were forming—lobsters, a covered bridge, flags, maple syrup, a white church spire, Pilgrims and turkeys, snowmen, moose, a red rooster, a scarlet leaf, the Mayflower, a granite face.

Then the stories came. You learned about Native American heroes and battles, pirates and patriots, poets and authors of spooky tales. The icons of New England, whether you live here on not, took residence in your mind. If the historic dates and flowery poems failed to stick, the images did not. This is a book filled with those familiar images.

New England, as the name implies, carries deep memories of its English origins. Yet it was the New England colonies that first threw out their British rulers in a painful burst of independence. The road to American democracy was no superhighway. It was as rocky and circuitous as a sleepy Yankee road. It was about idealism and faith, but it was also about economics and hard work. The story is not as simple as a child's puzzle map or as pretty as a poster.

But the land is. When you study the images in this book, one theme cuts through—how beautiful. We see why European settlers stayed and why the original Americans resisted. We understand why citizens of the first colonies struggled to create a government unknown in their time—a free people in an independent land. Like New England and its ecosystems, democracy is a complex structure with a simple beauty. It is as diverse as the seasons, as clear as a mountain view, as right as an April rain—and it feels like home.

Acknowledgment

This book represents the best of the best. After exploring New England in depth, town by town, we finally have a chance to step back and enjoy the beauty of our entire region.

As always, we offer our deepest thanks to the talented photographers who made this book possible. Twin Lights Publishers is continually amazed by the quality and quantity of images submitted to our photo contests. We are especially indebted to our "old friends" from New England who have been submitting pictures since this series began. Their work, and their enthusiastic support of our mission, proves we are on the right track.

Special thanks to our panel of judges who had the most difficult task of all—picking the winning entries. Determining what is definitively New England from this phenomenal body of scenic work was no "walk in the park." For us, certainly, all of the photos are winners, and we know you will enjoy them and share them for years to come.

Our thanks also to designer Sara Day of SYP Design & Production, Inc. in Cambridge, MA and author J. Dennis Robinson of SeacoastNH.com in Portsmouth, NH. Their combined skills complement the extraordinary images to create a treasured new collection.

JUDGES

Elizabeth Leahy is a graphic artist and photographer now living in Rockport, Massachusetts. A graduate of Skidmore College, Beth has worked for design firms, magazines and newspapers on both the East and West Coast. For the past twenty years her award-winning designs and photographs have appeared in numerous publications.

Sara Day creates book designs for source and educational book publishers, as well as elegant promotional materials and web designs. Co-owner of SYP Design & Production, Inc., Sara has designed a number of photographic journals that have made the essence of some of the most beautiful places in the world available to everyone. Ms. Day makes her home in Wenham, MA.

Warren Salinger's career has included a twenty year stint as an international development officer. He is a published author with a wide range of photographic experiences throughout the world. He has supervised two other "photographic portrait series" publications and splits his time between Rockport, MA and Gold Canyon, AZ.

FIRST PLACE

Light on the Rocks
ROBERT MULLARKEY

As the low afternoon light turns the sky to haze, architecture and environment reach complete harmony. In one flowing image, the photo-realism of the rocky Maine coast appears to morph into a watercolor painting of Bass Headlight.

Bob Mullarkey of Newburyport, MA caught the shutter bug at age14. He honed his craft as a loyal camera club member, attending workshops and field trips. He eventually won over 350 ribbons and dozens of trophies and medals competing with fellow members. Bob says he is "not much on people pictures," preferring land and seascapes. "To get the award-winning pictures, you have to get up before sunrise and get out on your own. You have to be tough on yourself," he says. Just retired from his career as a machinist, Bob now expects to see even more New England sunrises through a lens.

Life and Death

DOUGLAS R. AMENDE

A brilliant population of creeping phlox spreads like a carpet over the bones of two early Americans. The thriving "cemetery moss" seems to prefer life in the most ancient of New England's cemeteries.

Largely self-taught, Douglas AmEnde actually began his scenic work as an illustrator. A prolific shooter for 20 years, his archives include thousands of New England images. Guarding his secret shooting sites, Doug says this award-winning photo was taken at an old Connecticut cemetery in May. As director of an insurance company and the father of two, he works photography around a busy schedule. Doug's work has recently appeared in Cape Cod Life *and on the cover of* Downeast Magazine. *He is currently working on a complete book of Cape Cod photos.*

Time Flies *(opposite)*

MICHAEL HUBLEY

Crouched amid an 11-acre expanse of New Hampshire lupines, the photographer twists, stoops, brackets, and frames roll after roll of film. Suddenly, in the corner of one eye, a tiger swallowtail appears, and just as quickly, is gone.

At work, Michael Hubley touches up client graphics and photography using high-tech digital technology for a Massachusetts firm. Off work, he is free to follow his artistic dreams. His prize winning shot combined skill and luck. "I've never seen a butterfly while shooting at Sugar Hill," he says. "I set up my tripod and got one shot off before it flew away." That single frame captured an instant in time. Hubley's photo hobby is evolving toward a career, he says. His framed photos hang in a number of galleries. His work is featured on the covers of the Newburyport and White Mountains books in this series.

Connecticut

The Constitution State

Two White Chairs

CAROLE DRONG

New York City dwellers dream of such scenes. Two white chairs lounge by a rugged stone wall, reflected in the pond below. They seem to be waiting, beckoning perhaps, to a pair of harried urban souls.

Squash Match

ERNEST PICK

In Weston, CT, the natives take their
pumpkin competition seriously.
Contestants hang out here at the
Pumpkin Patch and size each other
up prior to the main event and
the coveted blue ribbon ceremony
that follows.

Eastern Charm *(opposite)*

CAROLE DRONG

Yankee ingenuity affords New
Englanders the license to adopt
and adapt all architectural forms.
This weathered building in Mystic
stands pagoda-like against an
autumn backdrop.

Our Founding Feathers *(left)*

CAROLE DRONG

All dressed for dinner, this trio is fixin' for a memorable Thanksgiving in New Preston. But first, these turkeys will attend an animal rights protest rally at Lake Waramaug. Birds are people too, you know.

Rise and Falls *(opposite)*

CAROLE DRONG

19th century New England was a pulsing industrial center. Black smoke belched from great brick factories that rose above hundreds of rushing streams. Then industry largely went South, often leaving only the sleek scenic water line like here at Cargill Falls in Putnam.

Udderly Fascinating *(above)*

DOUGLAS R. AMENDE

Haven't you herd? News travels fast around the barnyard. The arrival of a local photographer always draws a nosy crowd at this Stafford farm.

Colonial Survival

BILL CRNKOVICH

Before the Pilgrims landed at
Plymouth, traders were already
navigating the Connecticut River
in search of Native goods. Today
restored colonials remind residents
in the Constitution State of the days
when their ancestors were proud
British citizens.

Berry-Berry Good

DOUGLAS R. AMENDE

Native strawberries offer themselves up for harvest in South Windsor. Pick-your-own stands attract visitors who crave the full tactile, olfactory and gustatory experience. And those few free stolen bites are always the sweetest.

Gothic Revival *(above)*

DOUGLAS R. AMENDE

Wealthy Woodstock summer residents in the 19th century prefered their gardens ornate and their houses Gothic. Roseland Cottage, complete with ice-house, carriage house and private bowling alley, represents the best of times back in 1846.

Mock Medieval *(left)*

DAVID F. GOUVEIA

Eccentric actor William Gillette built this medieval-looking stone castle for a million dollars in 1919. Recently restored for nearly $12 million, its 24 rooms offer panoramic views of the Connecticut River at this state park in East Haddam.

Bridge Work *(above)*

JAMES BLANK

Few structures in the state have worked harder than this covered bridge spanning the Housatonic River in West Cornwall. Built in 1841, it has been in continuous use since the Civil War. Today cars still cross the 242-foot span.

Connecticut Cover *(left)*

CAROLE DRONG

Vermont may get most of the credit, but covered bridges still survive in every New England state. The Comstock Bridge, for example, was originally built in 1873 and dramatically spans 110 feet of the Salmon River.

Old Buttercup

DOUGLAS R. AMENDE

Near South Windsor horses graze in a field of flowers. This pastoral scene is a common sight in a state known for fine equine farms, frequent animals fairs and horseback riding, the sport of kings.

Wheel of Fortune

DOUGLAS R. AMENDE

Down by the old millstream is much more than a barbershop tune. A surprising number of restored mills survive today as tourist attractions. Once they operated saws, ground flour and powered factories, as Americans grew increasingly self-reliant.

Free Therapy *(opposite)*

FRANK KACZMAREK

In search of inner peace, consumers today spend millions on therapeutic massage, aroma therapy and soothing New Age recordings. But Mother Nature still does it best, and here at a brook near Lyme, does it for free.

The Weight of Water

CAROLE DRONG

A crafty Yankee reporter sent to cover
a great ice storm in 1886 conducted an
experiment. He weighed a small fallen
branch of 40 ounces, then melted away
its icy coating. The twig beneath it all
weighed only a single ounce.

Coventry Cathedral *(opposite)*

DOUGLAS R. AMENDE

In Coventry, England the arched ruins
of a medieval cathedral still survive
after a thousand years. In Coventry,
Connecticut, this fragile winter chapel
appears and disappears each winter
without the touch of a human hand.

Joseph Conrad

DOUGLAS R. AMENDE

More than 4,000 cadets trained on this ship before it came permanently to the Connecticut coast. Almost broken up in the 1930s, the Joseph Conrad made a 58,000-mile voyage around the world before arriving here at its final mooring at Mystic in 1947.

Op Sail *(opposite)*

CAROLE DRONG

Americans are rediscovering the age of sail. A recent Op Sail celebration brought together some of the finest rigged ships on the oceans today. Ships like Amistad, Gloria, and Eagle drew thousands to Connecticut ports.

New England's Rising Star *(above)*

DOUGLAS R. AMENDE

Modern Hartford at sunset is a far cry from the city Mark Twain adopted in the mid-19th century. Twain's unique mansion, his bit of heaven on Earth, is among the nation's most compelling literary tours.

Grand Old State *(left)*

JAMES BLANK

It isn't hard to tell that the architect of the Connecticut state capitol also designed cathedrals. The high Victorian Gothic style capitol of white marble and red slate was completed in 1878.

Riverfront Recapture *(opposite)*

THOMAS ROTKIEWICZ

Today the Connecticut River is alive with music, dance, ships and events. The restored stretch between Hartford and East Hartford includes a river walk, an amphitheater, parks, boat docks, wharves, and here, the band shell Riverside Plaza.

The Age of Sail

TERRY KLEIN

Like its coastal sister states,
Connecticut was tied to the sea during the age of sailing ships. Today,
spectacular events like Op Sail here
in New London, continue that rich
maritime history.

Hull of a School *(opposite)*

CYNTHIA CRONIG

Mystic Seaport is all about education.
Adjacent to the ropewalk building,
wooden dories are stacked in antici-
pation of the newest nautical trainees.
For a sailor, no amount of book-
learning, ultimately, can match the
lessons taught by the sea.

Rhode Island

The Ocean State

Amber Waves

HARRY LICHTMAN

Many visitors come to Sakonnet Point near Little Compton for views of its manmade lighthouse. But those working to save Narragansett Bay suggest that the natural beauty is the region's greatest asset. Walk through the fields and crouch by the rocks with a pair of binoculars to see seals at play far from the madding crowds.

Endangered Icons

DOUGLAS R. AMENDE

The earliest lighthouses were little more than lanterns hung on a pole. Although most structures are no longer owned or maintained by the US Coast Guard, nearly 200 survive along the New England coast. An endangered symbol of the region, lighthouses are largely supported today by a variety of private, public and nonprofit enthusiasts. A museum here in North Light on Block Island tells the story.

Block Island Light

DOUGLAS R. AMENDE

It may be the highest lighthouse in New England, but a plane or a boat is required to see it close-up. Most visitors decompress with a relaxing ferry ride to secluded 7,000-acre Block Island. To relax even more, leave the car behind and, once on-island, rent a bike or moped—or best—walk.

Sea-Green Rockers *(above)*

DOUGLAS R. AMENDE

On Block Island you can easily lose 100 years among the Victorian buildings and the cool salt breeze. You can catch the scent of wild roses and beach plums as the 21st-century sounds disappear beneath the endless pounding surf.

Light Housekeeping *(left)*

HELEN EDDY

This unique brick Victorian lighthouse was moved in the 1990s. After a century of Block Island erosion, 300 feet of cliff had disappeared, leaving the house teetering just 55 feet from the crashing waves.

Stairway to Heaven *(opposite)*

DOUGLAS R. AMENDE

Like an abstract painting, this wooden stairway leads from Monhegan Bluff near Block Island to the beach below. Beautiful Block Island is distinctive for two offshore lighthouses, one of which has been moved inland from the eroding bluffs.

Geometric Passage

DAVID E. JORDAN

Triangles converge on Narragansett Bay
as an America's Cup class sloop glides
beyond the tower of Castle Hill light.
Refreshing breezes, historic sites and a
beautiful coastline makes Newport,
according to many, the sailing capital
of the world.

Relaxing Paws

MICHAEL HUBLEY

Taking a paparazzi break, a shy polar bear hangs out in Providence. The photographer caught this candid moment at Roger Williams Park Zoo, he says, only after many hours of patient watching.

Ballooning Capitol *(above)*

JANE PEDESEN

New Englanders are, by nature, political. Living at the heartland of the nation's original colonies, Yankees accept, even welcome, a certain amount of hot air in government. Here, however, no metaphor is intended, as a Providence balloon festival heats up.

Wooden Welcom *(left)*

DEBORAH L. DIAMOND

Walking the streets of Newport should be good for college credit in architecture. While most "wooden cities" in New England burned or have been destroyed by urban renewal, many textbook 18th-century structures survive here. In the "Hill" and "Point" districts alone, 83 classic buildings are preserved.

Big Pricetag, Little State

HELEN EDDY

By the time the Rhode Island capitol was completed in 1904 the bill came to $3,018,416.33. Some 15 million bricks and 327,000 cubic feet of white Georgia marble were used. Visitors should not miss the historic cannon inside the entrance, the elegant state library and the stunning paintings and carvings on the inner dome.

Ocean Drive *(top)*

GORDON MATIJASEVIC

It's just another little cottage by the sea, in Newport anyway. Visitors be prepared to gawk as you navigate the 9 1⁄2 mile-scenic drive that winds among the craggy Atlantic coastline.

Castle Hill Light *(bottom)*

DEBORAH L. DIAMOND

It appears to grow directly from the jutting rocky ledge at the eastern entrance to Narragansett Bay. Automated in 1957, the handsome granite lighthouse offers a panoramic view just a short walk from Newport's Castle Hill Inn.

Mill on the Move *(opposite)*

JAMES BLANK

Visitors to Prescott Farm in Middleton see this 1812 windmill at home on the restored farm museum. But this rare two-stone grinding machine has been around. From its original home in Warren, the mill was moved to Fall River, Massachusetts. It was then moved to two locations in Portsmouth, RI. Idle in the 20th century, the Newport Restoration Foundation saved the old building in 1969—and moved it one last time.

Renaissance City *(top)*

HELEN EDDY

Founder Roger Williams would be proud. Providence is in tip-top shape as a cultural center these days. It's home to the best schools and a well-respected newspaper. But having a prime-time television show named in its honor—now that's status.

Playing Marbles *(bottom)*

BILL CRNKOVICH

Marble House was built in Newport between 1888 and 1892 by William K. Vanderbilt as a 39th birthday gift to his wife. $7 million of the $11 million spent on the summer mansion went toward the purchase of 500,000 cubic feet of marble. Its creation helped transform the quiet summer colony of wooden houses to the legendary resort of stone palaces. The couple, however, divorced in 1895.

100% Cotton *(opposite)*

JAMES BLANK

It was a radical idea back in 1790. Could water power be harnessed to drive a cotton spinning factory? The success of Slater Mill sparked new technology around New England at the dawn of the industrial age. Mill owners also copied the Rhode Island idea of using women and children as cheap labor for up to 16 hours a day. Now restored to the year 1830, this Pawtucket museum tells the whole cotton story.

This Old Mansion *(above)*

GORAN MATIJASEVIC

In Rhode Island, Newport is a metaphor for wealth. But the city is much more than mansions and yachts. "America's First Resort" also offers elegant dining, fine art museums, and, of course, shopping. Then it's back to the little bungalow in time to pull up the drawbridge and enjoy a nightcap.

Vander-Built *(left)*

DAVID E. JORDAN

The Breakers is the grandest of Newport's summer cottages and a symbol of the Vanderbilt family's social and financial preeminence at the turn of the 20th century. This opulent 70-room Italian Renaissance site opened to the public in 1948.

Goodnight Sweet Day *(above)*

DAVID E. JORDAN

It's been a busy day of mansion tours, fine food and historic architecture. Tomorrow there's a cliff walk along the eastern shore and a visit to historic Fort Adams. But for now, enjoy a sunset, and a nightcap in old Newport.

Watch Hill *(left)*

THOMAS ROTKIEWICZ

Precisely halfway between the bustle of Boston and the bustle of New York City is this tranquil spot. In Watch Hill on a clear day views of Block Island are stunning and the sunsets are legendary. Here on a sunny porch, the sky and the sea align in perfect balance.

Massachusetts

The Bay State

Name That Cliff

DEBORAH L. DIAMOND

The Algonquians called them Aquinniuh.
The first European tourist in 1602 called
them Dover Cliffs after the chalky white
cliffs of England. In 1662 a traveler
described the gaily colored Cape Cod
bluff as the "English gayhead" and that
name stuck.

Perfect Storm Harbor

JAMES BLANK

The true history of the New England coast is best expressed here in the fishing capital at Gloucester. This industry, more than any other, drew Europeans to brave the dangerous transatlantic voyage. Today the image of the Gloucester fisherman in the yellow slicker is known around the world. His statue still dominates a harbor thick with fishing trawlers and a sky flecked with eager gulls.

Rockport Sunday

JAMES BLANK

New Englanders remember a brilliant guitar solo from the early 1970s called "Rockport Sunday." Without a word, folk composer Tom Rush translated the feeling of this harbor with its wooden docks, warm sunshine, and hovering gulls.

Jaws Revenge

DEBORAH L. DIAMOND

The fictional shark in the film *Jaws*
never actually terrorized swimmers in
the waters off Cape Cod. But there
are plenty of big ferocious fish here
that attract schools of deep-sea
anglers, as here in Provincetown.

History for Sale *(top)*

DEBORAH L. DIAMOND

Brimfield is brimful of antiques. According to its organizers, this tri-annual event is the largest outdoor antiques show in the world. Over 6,000 dealers from around the world display their wares on 23 separate fields in three week-long extravaganzas.

Buoys Night Out *(bottom)*

DAVID E. JORDAN

Seafood lovers crave New England, traveling great distances for the freshest catch of the day. It doesn't get much fresher than Orleans, smack in the "elbow" of Cape Cod. Here in Rock Harbor, dinner practically leaps off the boats and into the tartar sauce.

White Elephant Safari *(above)*

DOUGLAS R. AMENDE

This is where the bargain hunters roam. Into the darkest reaches of the furthest rooms they search—relentless—alert to any sight or scent of a possible trophy. Spying one, the hunter freezes, scans the field for competitors. Then reaches for a wallet, unlocks the trigger and — CHARGES!

Visitors Welcome *(left)*

DAVID E. JORDAN

Since the dawn of tourism, the seaside town on Cape Ann has been welcoming visitors. Besides its many beaches, a glassy cove and harbor filled with boats—Rockport is a place of vivid colors. Artists have adopted the scenic fishing town and galleries abound.

Not Your Typical Oil Town

DOUGLAS R. AMENDE

Most early American oil towns are marked with towering rigs, but not Edgartown. Its wealth came from the sea during the hey-day of the New England whaling industry. Today the elegant Martha's Vineyard town is noted for the Greek revival homes built by wealthy whaling captains.

Storm Warning

MARSHA AND CHARLES KESSLER

Clichés carry more than a modicum of truth. New England weather is every bit as fickle as they say. A storm can threaten all day and never arrive, then the minute you turn your back, it hits like a rogue wave. Hear at Gay Head the sun plays peek-a-boo with a cliff-side lighthouse.

Quiet Harbor

DEBORAH L. DIAMOND

Ultimately this is what it's all about. A life of toil and noise and stress melts from memory when the travelers arrive. The boat moored, the sail hauled in, they take the skiff slowly along the white beach and disappear into a perfect Chatham day.

Pilgrim Sail

STANLEY CRONIG

It was not a good ride. Visitors who tour the *Mayflower II* learn of the enormous hardships of the Pilgrims' 1620 voyage. The full-scale reconstruction is harbored today three miles north of historic Plimouth Plantation's Eel River site near the legendary Plymouth Rock.

Gay Head *(above)*

DEBORAH L. DIAMOND

A sharp rock juts toward the setting sun off the coast of Martha's Vineyard. Like a sounding whale or sinking submarine, it breaks the glowing horizon in a surreal image that appears more imagined than seen.

Longfellow Bridge *(left)*

JAMES BLANK

Locals call them "salt and pepper shakers." The ancient-looking columns span the Charles River from Boston to Cambridge. The scenic memorial honors the Maine-born poet who turned Paul Revere and Hiawatha into household names.

Massachusetts Justice *(opposite)*

RODNEY R. HARRIS

The American Revolution began as a rejection of British law in which colonists, dressed as Native Americans, tossed the King's tea into the brink. Today federal judges can look down from a sweeping hall of glass 88 feet high when they need to remember how it all began.

New Kid on the Block *(opposite)*

JAMES BLANK

This is not the famous 1713 "Old Statehouse," Boston's oldest surviving public building. Beantown's "new" State House was built in 1798 on Beacon Hill on land owned by John Hancock. Designed by Charles Bulfinch, the shiny dome, once made of wooden shingles, now glows with 23-carat gold.

Ebb Tide

DOUGLAS R. AMENDE

A true Yankee craves a wooden boat, worn in all the right places, tested and true. "If God had intended fiberglass boats, he would have made fiberglass trees," the saying goes. But every boat must have its day. Here two elderly craft await renewal near a spray of lilies in Chatham.

It Peaked Early *(above)*

ROBERT V. BEHR

A fragile wire fence topped in fresh snow frames the summit of Mt. Greylock. At 3,491 feet, this point marks the highest elevation in Massachusetts. But when ranked against its lofty neighbors, Greylock does not even appear on the Top 100 list of New England's tallest peaks.

The Old Way

PAUL WATSON

Today many sap farmers tap their trees with plastic hoses and pull the sap into great vats with a noisy generator pump. Others prefer the ancient way. In the crisp morning, you can hear the farmer's footsteps through the woods. The buckets clank together and then the watery sap floods. This is all the sound you hear, repeated tree to tree.

Old North Bridge

ROBERT MULLARKEY

America the colony began in Jamestown, Virginia, at Plymouth Plantation, in early Florida, along Maine trading outposts and in Hudson Bay. But America the country began here on a little wooden bridge in Concord. Here legend says the shot heard 'round the world rang out and echoes still.

The Real Harvest

DOUGLAS R. AMENDE

Massachusetts is Thanksgiving. Although the holiday as we know it was created in the 19th century and bears little resemblance to the Pilgrim celebration—the legends stick. Besides wild turkey the feast included cod, bass, deer and waterfowl, plus meal and Indian corn.

Colrain Color (opposite)

DOUGLAS R. AMENDE

Sometimes the brilliance can overwhelm. The rods and cones in the human eye can barely take in what the brain can scarcely process. It's fall in New England, and when the air is crisp and the scent of wood smoke curls in on a crisp autumn day, you can't ever imagine being anywhere else.

Edgartown Harbor *(top)*

DAVID F. GOUVEIA

Many who love Cape Cod find its
essence in Edgartown. They mention
the clean island air, rambling bicycle
paths, narrow streets, brick sidewalks
and expansive views with a classic
white lighthouse.

Gingerbread Cottage *(bottom)*

DOUGLAS R. AMENDE

The architecture of Martha's Vineyard
cannot be easily pigeonholed.
Colonial saltboxes, federal-style,
Greek revival and shingle-style
homes abound. Still the Camp
Ground trend of Oak Bluffs stands
out with its bold colors and decora-
tive jigsaw-cut designs.

Alternative Energy

JAMES BLANK

Windmills appeared in New England and especially across Cape Cod as early as the 1600s. Jutting into the Atlantic, the Cape was ideal for its breezes that drove heavy wooden arms and turned massive grist stones for grinding. Later lighter windmills like this one in Chatham still survive.

Horseshoe House *(above)*

NANCY ROBISON

When the oldest house on Nantucket was struck by lightning in 1987, it did more damage than 301 years of previous history. Nicknamed for the horseshoe shape on its chimney, the lucky Coffin house was rebuilt and re-opened to public tours.

Bring on Winter *(left)*

DAVID E. JORDAN

There was a time when surviving a New England winter meant filling the woodshed with cords of crisp wood. That life survives at Sturbridge Village, a reconstructed New England town that never seems to change.

Heavenly Aspirations *(opposite)*

ROBERT V. BEHR

The classic New England valley town is sheltered in a ring of hills, its white church steeple pointing toward heaven. That postcard image is nowhere more familiar than in the Berkshires. Here the Congregational Church of Wiliiamstown extends skyward.

The Original Mayflower *(above)*

PAUL WATSON

A carpet of mayflowers spreads beneath the towering pines of Maudsley State Park in Newburyport. Once a 19th century estate, the buildings are gone and only a whisper of the formal gardens remain among stretches of mountain laurel. Most breathtaking are the ornamental trees and masses of azaleas and rhododendrons.

A Blooming Bridge

DOUGLAS R. AMENDE

In 1908 it was a trolley bridge. Today over 500 varieties of flowers and vines keep the 400-foot span in bloom from April through October. Located on the scenic Mohawk Trail in the Berkshire foothills, the "Bridge of Flowers" is supported by donations and lovingly maintained by the Shelburne Falls Women's Club.

Bogged Up

DAVID E. JORDAN

Farmed since 1880, the cranberry bogs
of Harwich are preserved forever as
part of a conservation trust. The town's
10-day Cranberry Festival is among
Cape Cod's biggest summer events.

New Hampshire

The Granite State

Fall River

HARRY LICHTMAN

Leaves blaze along the rushing
Ammonoosuc River in Bretton
Woods, New Hampshire. It is a scene
unchanged since the earliest New
England inhabitants gave the river its
name thousands of years ago.

Wild Lupine *(opposite)*

ROBERT J. KOZLOW

While the New Hampshire state flower is the glorious purple lilac, its color and beauty is challenged by the wild lupine, a member of the pea family. This stately and endangered species is celebrated each spring at a festival here in Sugar Hill in the White Mountain region.

Two if by Sea

HARRY LICHTMAN

Whaleback Light in Portsmouth Harbor stands behind New Castle Light in this dramatic and rare view. New Hampshire's only off-shore lighthouse on White Island is 10 miles out to sea. Buffeted by wind, sun and icy salt spray, the Isles of Shoals light is currently endangered.

Recovered Bridge

SCOTT D. CONNER

The first Albany Bridge went down in
an 1858 windstorm. It was rebuilt for
$1,300, minus expenses for the first
bridge, of course. Today, reinforced
by steel, it spans 120 feet across the
Swift River.

Rural Oyster River *(opposite)*

HARRY LICHTMAN

Durham was among the original five
New Hampshire "plantations" including Exeter, Portsmouth, Hampton and
Dover. In 1866 this farming commu-
nity became home to the University
of New Hampshire, originally an agri-
cultural school. Despite an under-
graduate population of over 10,000,
Durham still retains its rural charm.

Kancamagus Byway

STEVE VANCE

Locals call it "The Kanc" and it ranks among the National Scenic Byways. It climbs to nearly 3,000 feet alongside Mt. Kancamagus, winding through coniferous forests. Along the Swift River the foliage display offers some of the most diverse leafy colors in the world.

100 Waterfalls *(opposite)*

JANE PEDERSEN

Sabbaday Falls is among the most popular and accessible of over 100 waterfalls in the White Mountains. Visitors reach the cold, fresh 50-foot cascade by hiking just a few minutes off the Kancamagus Highway, one of the nation's most scenic drives.

Fort Point Light

HARRY LICHTMAN

New Hampshire has just one mainland lighthouse along its brief 18-mile coastline. Here in Newcastle, locals say, the first shots of the American Revolution were fired as 400 residents took control of Fort William and Mary six months before the battles at Lexington and Concord.

Habitat Not for Humanity

HARRY LICHTMAN

The 1,000-acre wildlife refuge in Jefferson is one of the newest in the nation. Here by Big and Little Cherry ponds, live voles, mice, moose, and bobcat roam. Over 200 species of birds have been spotted along the wetlands among spruce, pine, balsam fir, ash and cherry.

Ethereal Waterway

HARRY LICHTMAN

Ossipee Lake seems to hover above the trees in a surreal pallet of sunset colors. This view comes from the hills of Effingham where fire tower volunteers scan the fiery fall horizon for hints of an actual blaze.

Dawn of Time *(opposite)*

HARRY LICHTMAN

It looks like the cover of a book on the history of the universe and in a sense, it is. Each morning the Earth strikes dawn, and while great hoards of tourists sleep nearby, the sun recalls a day when no eyes blinked and no hearts stirred, a time when life itself was eons yet to come.

Sunset Over Rye, NH

HARRY LICHTMAN

As the day ends the harbor goes to glass and the sun paints the last of the high clouds pink, then scarlet, then orange. This is when the gulls find their way home and the last of the evening sailboats glide silently toward the sheltering cove.

Slide of Frankenstein *(opposite)*

HARRY LICHTMAN

Hikers may approach Arethusa Falls from the Frankenstein Trail. The monstrous drop of 170 feet makes it the tallest falls in the state and a spectacular sight. Ice climbers scale the frozen falls, a bizarre winter scene to watch.

Rusticating in Tamworth

ROBERT J. KOZLOW

There ought to be a law against getting more picturesque than little Tamworth. From the late 1800s "rusticators" from the city have made their way to this isolated village that still operates at a 19th-century pace. In the evening, visitors may still hear the strains of a fiddle band and the thump of country dancers in the town meeting hall.

Presidential Aspirations *(top)*

HARRY LICHTMAN

It's the big climb. Hikers yearn to master the campaign trails of Jefferson, Madison, Adams and the 6,288-foot Mt. Washington. Hard to believe, on a balmy day, that the world's record winds of 231 mph were recorded here. More than 20 feet of snow falls annually, and still the climbers come.

Reading Room *(bottom)*

ROBERT J. KOZLOW

It's a moderate-to-easy three-mile hike, according to the guidebook, although steep toward the finale but the panoramic view of Lake Winnipesaukee makes it all worthwhile. NH peaks, like here on the summit of Mt. Major, are among the state's most popular attractions.

Cathedral Ledge *(opposite)*

KEVIN AND SUSAN PSAROS

Despite the mounting death toll, climbers literally stand in line to ascend 700-foot Cathedral Ledge. The day-long climb offers spectacular views of Echo Lake in Conway below. The same view is available to visitors who opt to take the much safer auto road to the top.

Old Granite Jaw *(top)*

TERRY WEDDLETON

No collection of New Hampshire images is complete without the stony stare of the Old Man of the Mountains. The 40-foot optical illusion on Profile Mountain is a traffic stopper in Franconia Notch. Daniel Webster, another "Old Stone Face" from the region, said it was a sign that God made New Hampshire men rugged.

The Summit Seeker *(bottom)*

DAVID E. JORDAN

The original cog railroad is now the only steam engine of its kind. Begun in 1869 with "Old Peppersass," the Cog Railway now operates seven engines that push visitors up Mt. Washington, New England's tallest peak. Each trip to the summit consumes over one ton of coal, and takes 1,000 gallons of water to move the 18-ton engine.

Autumn Sonata

MICHAEL HUBLEY

One can almost hear the music, Vivaldi's *Four Seasons* perhaps, or something woodsy by Grieg. The swirling leaves may suggest a Schumann waltz or the color bring Stravinsky's *Firebird Suite* to mind. But all we hear is the tapping of woodpeckers and the distant call of a loon.

Revolutionary Facts *(above)*

PAUL WATSON

More New Hampshire men fought at the "Battle of Bunker Hill" than residents of any other New England colony, a fact few know. Thousands of African Americans served in the Revolution too, although their descendants' freedom was 100 years in coming. Annually thousands attend this Exeter festival to discover more about the true nature of patriotism.

First in the Nation *(left)*

ROBERT J. KOZLOW

Once every four years the nation focuses on Dixville Notch where the first votes of the first presidential primary are cast at the stroke of midnight. The rest of the time, the Balsams is the main attraction in town. Established as the Dix House just after the Civil War, it remains one of New England's best known resorts.

Washington in Winter *(above)*

ROBERT BICKNELL

250 master craftsmen from Italy labored two years to open this remote hotel in 1902. It has been the symbol of New Hampshire hospitality for a century since. The Mount Washington Hotel opened for its first winter season in 1999.

Frosty Slopes *(right)*

ROBERT J. KOZLOW

Perhaps they should change the Granite State motto to "Live, Ski or Die." Today the region is synonymous with the sport and even boasts a new Ski Museum. The Flume Bridge in Lincoln is just a shush and a snowplow away from the Loon Mountain facility nearby.

Old Strawbery Banke

ROBERT J. KOZLOW

It was on these banks in 1630, historians believe, that the first Portsmouth settlers encamped. They did not come for religious freedom, but as workers for an English "corporation" that hoped to reap great profits from New England fish, timber and Indian trade. The New Hampshire investors never made much money, but descendants of the settlers still remain.

In Search of Sunny *(above)*

KEVIN AND SUSAN PSAROS

Passengers on a narrated river cruise learn the legend of a Loch Ness-style monster who reportedly lives in the depths of Lake Sunapee. "Sunny" is said to be a peaceful, monster who ranges the 10-mile lake, harming no one, and promoting local tourism.

The Big House *(left)*

TERRY WEDDLETON

With 400 elected officials meeting in Concord, New Hampshire claims the third largest legislative body in the English-speaking world. Only the US House of Representatives and the British Parliament have more representatives.

Not-so-Lonesome Lake

MICHAEL HUBLEY

1,000 feet above the floor of
Franconia Notch, Lonesome Lake is
rarely without friends and admirers.
Hikers on the Appalachian Trail stop
regularly for a snack and a photo,
take in the stunning view of Cannon
Mountain, and press on.

Cinematic Scenery *(opposite)*

ROBERT J. KOZLOW

Who can forget that scene in *On
Golden Pond* when Henry Fonda
takes an unplanned dip in his
favorite New Hampshire lake? That
scene was filmed somewhere here in
six-mile Squam Lake in Holderness.
As deep as 100 feet and fed by a
natural spring, lovely Squam passes
every screen test.

Maine

The Pine Tree State

Textbook Coast

DEBORAH L. DIAMOND

The rocky shore off Mt. Desert Island offers all that the name "Maine" conjures. Here the harsh cliffs meet the white-capped open sea. Brave pines stand guard between the curves of a small cove and the distant hills. All that's missing are a lobster and a moose.

Cape of the Winds *(opposite)*

MICHAEL LEONARD

President John Quincy Adams author-
ized the building of Owl's Head Light
in 1825. Although just 30 feet tall, it is
perched on a 100-foot promontory.
The lighthouse and surrounding State
Park is considered a must-see for lighthouse lovers.

Sailor's Take Warning *(above)*

AMY S. CAMPBELL

Scientists say a red sky appears when
the blue light has been reflected
away along that line of sight due to a
phenomenon called Rayleigh scatter-
ing. Sailors care only that the red
sunrise bodes danger. Lovers care
neither for reason nor prophecy, and
seize the romantic moment.

Lighthouse to the Stars *(above)*

TERRY KLEIN

Poet Sarah Orne Jewett, one of Maine's finest, was drawn to the Port Clyde area. Her classic *Country of the Pointed Firs* was written here. The Marshall House Lighthouse stood even then, and today houses a museum. Among its treasures is a photo of Tom Hanks, who visited during the filming of *Forrest Gump*. Stephen King's *Thinner* was filmed here too.

Ocean Fury *(left)*

LOU NOVICK

The life of a fisherman is not for most. They rise soon after we retire and trust themselves to the mercy of a some-times angry sea. The coast of New England is dotted with memorials to the farmers of this unpredictable field of blue.

Decisions, Decisions *(above)*

JAMES BLANK

What to do in New Harbor? Perhaps visit Pemaquid Point Light, site of so many dramatic shipwrecks. Or take the ferry to Monhegan Island where the cliffs rise from the sea. There are tour boats leaving to view colonies of puffins and seals. Or, perhaps, with a scene like this, it's better just to stand stock-still and pray for many more such days.

Thank a Glacier *(right)*

JAMES BLANK

Besides 3,500 miles of twisting coastline, Maine claims thousands of inland water bodies carved out by the last Ice Age. Sebago Lake, the deepest and second-largest, is active year-round near the foot of New Hampshire's White Mountains.

Settling In *(above)*

RAYMOND TURMELLE

All roads seem to lead to Camden for those driving the rocky coastal route of mid-Coast Maine. There's something welcoming here by the small harbor near the protected Camden Hills. With a population of just over 5,000 souls, Camden is now the region's retirement capital.

Arts and Crafts *(left)*

PAUL WATSON

For many, Bar Harbor is Maine. Its rock-bound coast and granite cliffs have been the focus of maritime painters since before the Civil War. Surrounded by the natural magic of Acadia the region once sported grand Victorian hotels, all of which are gone. But the charm remains, right down to the artsy shops.

Manana Hermitage *(opposite)*

KEVIN AND SUSAN PSAROS

From the dock at Monhegan Island in Casco Bay the tour guide points to nearby Manana Island and the tumbled home of the "Manana Hermit." Residents remember a gentle man, a New Yorker who grew tired of the city. He lived here until his 80s, not alone, but with twenty-three sheep and a big white duck named Donald.

Settling In *(above)*

Intersecting Seasons

MATT BROWN

When Fall is at play in Baxter State Park, winter has already begun at the peak of Mt. Katahdin. At 5,268 feet, Katahdin is the only mountain in the New England's Top 10 elevations not claimed by New Hampshire.

Slow Down *(left)*

WILLIAM MATTERN

A happy trend in tourism, more and more Maine visitors are trading in four wheels for two. Bicycle tours are the ultimate way to take in the vistas and villages like here at Port Clyde. Kayaking too is on the rise as travelers take to the waters for a slow sea-level perspective.

Classic New England *(opposite)*

SCOTT D. CONNER

This could be any New England state—a red barn and a white fence on a crisp winter day. The sky promises and threatens. The shadows lengthen and the circle of the seasons continues here in New Gloucester, Maine as it does throughout this beautiful region.

HONORABLE MENTION

The Bubbles

MICHAEL HUBLEY

There's no view like it in Acadia.
"The Bubbles" appear to percolate
from Jordan Lake where hikers catch
the trail that encircles the entire pond.
Located on the western side of Park
Loop Road, the two rounded mountains against the clear water are
considered among the most scenic
in Maine.

Rainbow Pond *(top)*

PAUL WATSON

An old folk saying goes: Rainbow to
windward, foul fall the day; Rainbow to
leeward, damp runs away. New England
wisdom also tells us—If there be a rainbow in the eve, it will rain and it will
leave. This stunning optical show was
captured over Sandy Stream Pond in
Baxter State Park. After the rain, as
promised, it left.

The Nesowadnehunk *(bottom)*

MATT BROWN

Today adventurers prize the stream for
challenging and spectacular whitewater
rafting. Earlier it was a logging camp. In
1930 Maine Governor Percival Baxter
"gave" more than 200,000 natural acres
to form Baxter State Park. But the Native
names along the Penobscott River
remind us of the people who lived here
more than 10,000 years before.

The Quiet Side *(above)*

STEVE BALLARD

The word most often used to describe the region is "quaint." Bass Harbor is located on what summer visitors call the "back" or "quiet" side of Mt. Desert Island. The more tourists discover Acadia National Park nearby, the more others search for the road less traveled—and find it here.

Maine Stratification *(left)*

KEVIN AND SUSAN PSAROS

The Creator has to draw a line somewhere. And here it is, in a sharply divided sky over the Island Inn on Monhegan. Luckily, this being an artist colony, there was a photographer handy to capture this definitive sunset.

Made in Maine *(above)*

JAMES BLANK

Behind every scenic port is a hard-knuckle town. Resettled by Scott and Irish immigrants after the early Indian wars, Boothbay had to develop its own commerce. Locally-built schooners carried Maine bricks and even ice to Boston and returned with coal and manufactured goods. During two World Wars, this peaceful harbor even built minesweepers—whatever it took to survive.

The All-American Lobster *(right)*

MELISSA STUFFLEBEAM

Indians used them for fertilizer. In Colonial times the bottom-feeding crustacean was the food of children, prisoners and the very poor. Today these ugly creatures are a delicacy. Maine is the largest lobster-producing state in the nation, as these traps at Mackerel Cove on Bailey Island show.

Odocoileus Virgianus

PAUL WATSON

Sleeping by day, feeding by night, deer can often be seen on Mount Derert Island at dawn.

Bull Wrinkle

PAUL WATSON

It's not easy being Maine's largest mammal, weighing up to half a ton. It takes a lot of tree buds to fuel a moose. Mating battles can be a real headache too. Maine's moose population has increased 15 times from what it was in 1900.

Beyond Walden Pond *(above)*

PAUL WATSON

We don't imagine him with a water bottle and hiking boots, but Henry David Thoreau was an avid hiker. He visited the distant stream at what is now Baxter State Park in 1846. Today hikers pick from among 37 marked tours, including Abol Trail that leads here to Thoreau Stream.

Toll Bridge *(right)*

STEVE VANCE

Of 120 covered bridges that once spanned the rivers of Maine, only eight original buildings survive. A precious few have been reconstructed. Fire, flood, ice, and the demands of progress have taken their toll.

The Frozen Couple *(above)*

AMY S. CAMPBELL

This icy Rockport image calls to mind the legend of an engaged couple, stranded on a capsizing boat three days before Christmas in 1850. Richard Ingraham and Lydia Dyer were discovered aboard the broken vessel, locked in a block of ice. Rescuers moved the heavy block to Owl's Head lighthouse. Thawed slowly, the pair revived, survived, married and had four children.

Anywhere, ME *(left)*

MATT BROWN

Maine is the most forested state in the nation—roughly 18 million wooded acres. With almost 90 percent of the state covered in trees, imagine finding your way out of this pine forest. Here the woods fill up with snow in Rangeley State Park.

Puffin Paradise

KEVIN AND SUSAN PSAROS

As you approach Machias Seal Island near New Brunswick, Canada, the air fills with birds, swooping and dipping into the sea for fish. Wardens limit the number of visitors on the protected area to reduce human impact to the wild population. Here 3,500 Atlantic puffins, Maine's largest gathering, live among terns, razorbills and murres.

Vermont

The Green Mountain State

Ethan Allen Highway

DARLENE BORDWELL

The Green Mountain boys roamed historic Route 7A when it was little more than a dirt cart path. Young vigilantes harassed the "city folk" from New York and made it clear that the New Republic was populated with independent-minded citizens. Vermonters were first to join the 13 colonies and first to outlaw slavery.

Horse Power

DOUGLAS R. AMENDE

A Vermont resident who got his first Model T found his animals were at odds with high technology. Five of his horses almost died in revenge, the old Yankee said. And when he started the new vehicle in the barn, the horses almost jumped into the hayloft.

Glass Falls

STEVEN J. BALLARD

In Quechee, Vermont an historic
woolen mill comes to life. But this
time the Ottauquechee River powers a
hydroelectric turbine that fuels a glass
furnace. Inside, teams of glassblowers
magically create designs for the Simon
Pearce company.

The Vermont Coast

JAMES BLANK

The days of smugglers hiding along Lake Champlain are done. Today Malletts Bay is encircled by summer camps and supports a small fleet of pleasure craft. Vermont's "inner coast" includes public swim beaches, a boating club, even a drive-in theater.

Rural Oyster River *(opposite)*

Less is More

JAMES BLANK

They call Montpelier "the smallest capital city in America" with pride. The streets are lit, the grass is green, and the people are friendly.

Agricultural Vision *(above)*

DAVID E. JORDAN

From the start Shelburne Farms was meant to be perfect. In 1886 the Webb family created a model farm on 3,800 acres. Everything was innovative, from the design of the buildings to the planting of crops and use of land. Today this preserved education center is among Vermont's top attractions.

White Horse Winner *(left)*

PAUL WATSON

The game plays out as the two children in the back seat keep score. They stare out competing windows, right and left. Each animal spotted equals five points. A herd of cows is a windfall. Any cemetery is a killer, setting the counter back to zero. Then one child shouts, "I win! I win!" It's a white horse, grazing in a distant field—and worth 500 points.

Delicate Balance *(opposite)*

JAMES BLANK

Perched above a river by a rushing mill pond, the Warren Lincoln Gap Bridge was recently restored to its 1880 design. A sixty-six foot piece of lumber replaced the bottom chord. The first car across after the ribbon cutting was a proud Model T.

Moss Glen Falls

DOUGLAS R. AMENDE

Just a few feet off Route 100 a wooden ramp leads visitors to the very edge of the falling water. Vermont's Granville Gulf Reservation offers hiking and fishing among hemlock and spruce near the headwaters of the White River. If that's not enough, a second waterfall with the same name can be found in Stowe.

Global Meltdown (opposite)

DOUGLAS R. AMENDE

It used to be a typical Spring thaw. Now scientists predict a four-degree rise in Vermont temperatures this century. A warmer climate would lead to an earlier snowmelt, causing dangerously higher streams, that then impact rivers. But it's still lovely, isn't it?

Winter Candle

RAYMOND TURMELLE

Vermont is the only New England state without a coastline. Yet at dusk, the steeple of this East Orange church glows like a lighthouse beacon against an ocean of fallen snow.

First Frost

ROBERT MULLARKEY

The tomatoes, thankfully, are covered
and the first cord of wood cut and
stacked. The big insects are suddenly
gone, but the first frost stirs the little
ones into a final frenzy. The pasture
too gives one last green burst while
the dogs, sensing winter, call to each
other across the crisp distance.

Honor Snacks

DOUGLAS R. AMENDE

Don't look for this self-service stand in New York City. Rural customers are invited to select their syrup and drop a payment into the bucket. Customers form a single line. No sticky fingers allowed. All goods must be consumed off premises. Flapjacks not included.

Sappy Shapes

DOUGLAS R. AMENDE

No matter how it's packaged, the world's best maple syrup comes from Vermont. Indians called it "drawn from the wood" and taught colonists how to cut trees, collect and cook the watery sap.

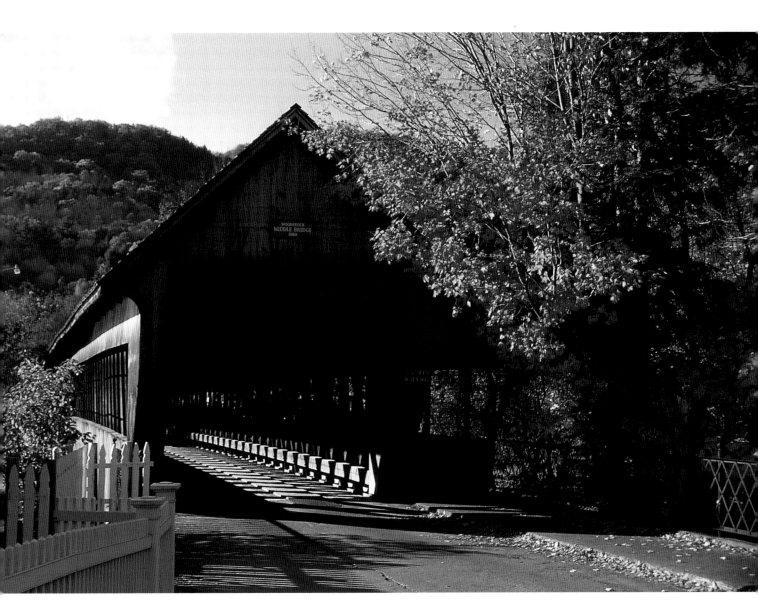

Wish Fulfillment

DAVID E. JORDAN

According to one Vermont historian, there's a foolproof way to make a wish come true while driving through a covered bridge. Compose the wish before entering, then lift your feet off the floor of the car and repeat "Bunny, bunny, bunny" all the way through. You must say "Rabbit" as you exit the far end. Happy results are guaranteed.

Up/Down Route 100

RODNEY R. HARRIS

It winds 200 miles North and South,
splitting the state as if chopped with
an ax. Just three stoplights and no fast
food joints interrupt this classic stretch
of road of old Vermont.

Twin Peaks

JAMES BLANK

Nothing says more about a Yankee man than his barn—someone once said—not his house, not his horse, not his kids or kin. It stands as he stands, tilts if he drinks, falls when he falters, and smells—well, you get the metaphor.

Counting Cows

JAMES BLANK

Vemont farmers produce more than two billion pounds of milk annually. They supply more maple syrup than any other state. The long list of key farm items includes apples, potatoes, eggs, honey, vegetables, Christmas trees, wood, and greenhouse nursery products. Amen.

Pickets Charged

DAVID A. KIRKWOOD

A white picket fence and an autumn tree near Bennington seem to glow with their own internal light.

Church and State *(opposite)*

JAMES BLANK

The Old First Church in Bennington is so central to local history that it was named "Vermont's Colonial Shrine" by the state legislature. The first Protestant meeting house in the state was erected here before the Revolution in 1763. This newer structure was dedicated in 1806. Poet Robert Frost and 75 veterans, many from the Battle of Bennington, are buried in the adjoining cemetery.

Contributors

Douglas R. AmEnde
79 Constance Drive
Manchester, CT 06040
6, 13, 15, 16, 18(2), 21, 23, 24,
30, 31, 32, 33, 50, 51, 57, 60,
61, 62, 66, 112, 118, 119, 122(2)

Steven J. Ballard
1153 Wheatsheaf Lane
Abington, PA 19001
104, 113

Robert V. Behr
PO Box 446
Williamstown, MA 01267
58, 65

Robert Bicknell
270 Hoyts Wharf Road
Groton, MA 01450
87

James Blank
1110 Red Maple Drive
Chula Vista, CA 91910
17, 24, 39, 41, 46, 47, 54, 56,
63, 97(2), 105, 114, 115, 117,
125, 126, 127

Darlene Bordwell
216 Goodell Road
Petersburgh, NY 12138
110–111

Matt Brown
45 Rustic Lane
Portsmouth, ME 04103
100, 103, 108

Amy S. Campbell
PO Box 659
Rockport, ME 04856
95, 108

Scott D. Conner
13612 Elena Gailegos Pl., N.E.
Alburquerque, NM 87111
72, 101

Bill Crnkovich
3225 W. Cameron Park Ct.
South Jordan, UT 84095
14, 40

Cynthia Cronig
47 Lakeside Drive East
Centerville, MA 02632
24

Stanley Cronig
47 Lakeside Drive East
Centerville, MA 02632
53(2)

Deborah L. Diamond
360 Gibbs Ave. #6
Newport, RI 02840
36, 38, 44–45, 48, 49, 52,
54, 92–93

Carole Drong
67 Hancock Drive
Mystic, CT 06355
8–9, 11, 12, 13, 17, 20, 22

Helen Eddy
26 Mt. Auburn Street
Cambridge, MA 02138
32, 37, 40

David F. Gouveia
Gov. Bradford Lane
Falmouth, MA 02540
16, 62

Rodney R. Harris
15 Vanderbilt Street
Randolph, MA 02368
55, 124

Michael Hubley
7 River Drive
Danvers, MA 01923
7, 35, 85, 90, 102

David E. Jordan
8 Echo Woods Road
Harwich, MA, 02645
34, 42, 43, 49, 50, 64, 67,
84, 116, 123

Frank Kaczmarek
11 Vermont Drive
Oakdale, CT 06370
19

Marsha and Charles Kessler
7969 Gunsmith Road
Houston, MN 55943
52

David A. Kirkwood
13 Stoneledge Drive
Portland, ME 04102
126

Terry Klein
67 Hancock Drive
Mystic, CT 06355
26, 96

Robert J. Kozlow
PO Box 905
Lincoln, NH 03251
70, 81, 82, 86, 87, 88, 91

Michael Leonard
68 Ledgewood Drive
Yarmouth, ME 04096
94

Harry Lichtman
39 Kimball Way
Newmarket, NH 03857
back jacket, 1, 28–29, 68–69, 71,
73, 76(2), 77, 78, 79, 80, 82

Goran Matijasevic
420 S. LA Esperanza
San Clemente, CA 92572
38, 42

William Mattern
429 Country Way
Scituate, MA 02066
100

Robert Mullarkey
20 Highland Ave
Newburyport, MA 01950
front jacket, 5, 59, 121

Lou Novick
800 NE 72 St
Miami, FL 33138
96

Jane Pedersen
5 Stowe Croft Dr.
Hampton, NH 03842
36, 75

Ernest Pick
4012 Bonita Avenue
Coconut Grove, FL 33133
10

Kevin and Susan Psaros
39 School Street
Melrose, MA 02176
83, 89, 99, 104, 109

Nancy Robison
34 Long Bay Dr.
Newport Beach, CA 92660
64

Thomas Rotkiewicz
65 Sheffield Drive
Windsor, CT 06095
25, 43

Melissa Stufflebeam
162 Oak Hill Rd
Litchfield, ME 04350
105

Raymond Turmelle
14 Green Hill Rd
Barrington, NH 03825
98, 120

Steve Vance
1283 Oak Lane
Herber City, UT 84032
74, 107

Paul Watson
70 Halls Mill Rd
Newfields, NH 038536
58, 66, 86, 98, 103, 106(2),
107, 116

Terry Weddleton
4 Freedom Circle #15
Portsmouth, NH 03801
84, 89